Table Of Contents

Chapter 2: The Impact of AI on Society...........................1

Chapter 3: Preparing for an AI-Driven Future 1

Chapter 4: AI in Personal Life 1

Chapter 5: Navigating Relationships with AI..................1

Chapter 6: Privacy and Security in an AI World 1

Chapter 7: Embracing Ethical AI 1

Chapter 8: The Future of AI 1

Chapter 9: Living Harmoniously with AI 1

Chapter 10: Action Steps for Today..................................1

Chapter 1: Understanding AI 2

Chapter 1: Understanding AI

The Basics of Artificial Intelligence

Artificial intelligence, commonly referred to as AI, represents a transformative technology that simulates human intelligence processes through the creation and application of algorithms. At its core, AI encompasses various capabilities, including learning from data, reasoning, problem-solving, and understanding natural language. These processes allow machines to perform tasks that traditionally required human intelligence, such as recognizing speech, making decisions, or translating languages. Understanding these fundamentals is crucial for individuals and organizations alike as they navigate an increasingly AI-integrated world.

There are several key types of AI, broadly categorized into narrow AI and general AI. Narrow AI, or weak AI, is designed to perform specific tasks, such as facial recognition or internet searches. This type of AI is prevalent in everyday applications like virtual assistants, recommendation systems, and automated customer service. In contrast, general AI, or strong AI, refers to a theoretical form of AI that possesses the ability to understand, learn, and apply intelligence across a wide range of tasks, similar to human cognitive abilities. While general AI remains largely a concept, advancements in narrow AI continue to evolve rapidly, influencing various sectors from healthcare to finance.

Machine learning is a critical subset of AI that focuses on developing algorithms that enable machines to learn from and make predictions based on data. Within machine learning, there are different approaches, including supervised learning, unsupervised learning, and reinforcement learning. Supervised learning involves training algorithms on labeled data, allowing them to make predictions or classifications. Unsupervised learning, on the other hand, deals with unlabeled data and aims to identify patterns or groupings. Reinforcement learning is characterized by its use of reward systems to encourage certain behaviors, effectively allowing machines to learn through trial and error.

The impact of AI on everyday life is profound and multifaceted. From smart home devices that enhance convenience to AI-driven medical diagnostics that improve patient outcomes, the integration of AI into daily activities is reshaping how individuals interact with technology. Moreover, AI is playing a pivotal role in optimizing business operations, enhancing customer experiences, and driving innovation across industries. As AI systems become more sophisticated, they are increasingly capable of handling complex tasks, leading to greater efficiency and productivity.

As society embraces the potential of AI, understanding its basics will empower individuals to adapt and thrive in this new landscape. Awareness of how AI functions, its capabilities, and its limitations can help alleviate fears and misconceptions surrounding the technology. Furthermore, preparing for a world dominated by AI involves not only embracing its benefits but also advocating for ethical practices and policies that ensure its responsible development and deployment. This proactive approach will enable everyone to harness AI's potential while safeguarding societal values and human well-being.

Different Types of AI

Artificial Intelligence (AI) encompasses a wide range of technologies and capabilities that can be categorized into different types based on their complexity and functionality. The most common classification divides AI into three main types: narrow AI, general AI, and superintelligent AI. Narrow AI, also known as weak AI, is designed to perform a specific task or a limited set of tasks. Examples include voice assistants like Siri and Alexa, recommendation algorithms used by streaming services, and image recognition software. These systems excel in their designated functions but lack the ability to perform beyond their programmed capabilities.

General AI, or strong AI, refers to a type of artificial intelligence that has the ability to understand, learn, and apply intelligence across a wide range of tasks, much like a human being. This type of AI is still largely theoretical and has not yet been achieved. Researchers and engineers are actively working toward developing systems that can reason, solve problems, and adapt to new situations in a way that mimics human cognitive abilities. The implications of general AI are profound; if created, it could transform various industries, enhance productivity, and even change the nature of human work.

Superintelligent AI is a concept that describes an AI system that surpasses human intelligence and capabilities in virtually every aspect. This type of AI, often depicted in science fiction, raises significant ethical and existential questions. While superintelligent AI is not currently a reality, discussions surrounding it emphasize the need for caution and responsible development practices as AI technology continues to advance. The potential for superintelligence to outstrip human control necessitates a proactive approach to AI governance and ethical considerations.

Another important distinction within AI is between reactive machines, limited memory, theory of mind, and self-aware AI. Reactive machines are the simplest form, responding to specific inputs without any memory or learning capability. Limited memory AI can use past experiences to inform future decisions, such as self-driving cars that adjust their behavior based on previous driving data. Theory of mind AI, which is still in the research phase, aims to understand and interpret human emotions and intentions. Lastly, self-aware AI would possess consciousness and self-awareness, allowing it to understand its own existence, which remains a speculative topic for the future.

As AI continues to evolve, understanding these different types and their implications is crucial for everyone. Awareness of how narrow AI impacts daily life, the potential of general AI to reshape industries, and the ethical discussions surrounding superintelligent AI can help individuals prepare for a future increasingly influenced by these technologies. By fostering a deeper understanding of AI's capabilities and limitations, society can better navigate the challenges and opportunities that lie ahead in a world where artificial intelligence plays an integral role in everyday life.

AI in Everyday Life

Artificial intelligence is increasingly becoming a part of our everyday lives, influencing how we work, communicate, and even make decisions. From virtual assistants like Siri and Alexa to smart home devices that learn our preferences, AI technology is designed to enhance convenience and efficiency. These systems analyze data to provide personalized experiences, making tasks such as managing schedules, controlling home environments, or even shopping more streamlined. Understanding the role of AI in our daily routines can help individuals harness its potential and mitigate any challenges it may present.

In the realm of communication, AI tools are transforming the way we interact. Chatbots and automated customer service systems are now commonplace on various platforms, offering immediate responses to inquiries and resolving issues without human intervention. This not only improves response times but also allows businesses to allocate human resources to more complex tasks. Additionally, AI-powered translation applications break down language barriers, enabling seamless communication across cultures. As these technologies continue to evolve, they promise to further enhance connectivity in an increasingly globalized world.

AI's impact extends into the workplace as well, where automation and machine learning are reshaping traditional job roles. Many industries are adopting AI to analyze data trends, optimize operations, and improve decision-making processes. While some fear that AI may lead to job displacement, it is important to recognize its potential to create new roles and opportunities. Workers can adapt by developing skills that complement AI technologies, focusing on creativity, critical thinking, and emotional intelligence—areas where human insight remains invaluable.

Health and wellness are other critical areas where AI is making significant inroads. Wearable devices that monitor health metrics, such as heart rate and activity levels, utilize AI to provide personalized feedback and recommendations. Telemedicine platforms use AI algorithms to assist in diagnosing conditions based on patient data, improving access to healthcare services. These advancements not only empower individuals to take control of their health but also enhance the overall efficiency of healthcare systems, allowing for quicker and more accurate patient care.

As AI continues to integrate into our daily lives, it is essential to remain informed and proactive. Awareness of the benefits and challenges associated with AI can help individuals make informed decisions about how to interact with these technologies. Embracing AI means not only leveraging its capabilities for personal and professional growth but also engaging in discussions about ethical considerations and data privacy. By preparing ourselves for a future intertwined with artificial intelligence, we can maximize its advantages while fostering a society that values both innovation and humanity.

Chapter 2: The Impact of AI on Society

AI in the Workforce

The integration of artificial intelligence into the workforce is reshaping industries and redefining the nature of work itself. AI technologies, including machine learning, natural language processing, and robotics, are being deployed to enhance productivity, streamline operations, and optimize decision-making processes. This shift is not just about replacing human labor but augmenting it, allowing workers to focus on more complex tasks that require creativity, empathy, and critical thinking. As AI continues to evolve, understanding its role in the workplace is essential for both employers and employees.

One of the most significant impacts of AI in the workforce is the automation of repetitive and mundane tasks. Routine activities, such as data entry, scheduling, and inventory management, are increasingly handled by AI systems, freeing up human workers to engage in more strategic and creative endeavors. This transition can lead to increased job satisfaction and efficiency, as employees can concentrate on high-value work that leverages their unique skills. However, it also raises concerns about job displacement and the need for reskilling the workforce to adapt to new roles that emerge from this technological shift.

Moreover, AI is enhancing decision-making processes by providing data-driven insights that were previously unattainable. Businesses can analyze vast amounts of data quickly, identifying trends and patterns that inform strategic decisions. This capability allows organizations to respond more swiftly to market changes and consumer demands. As AI tools become more sophisticated, they will play an integral role in strategic planning, risk assessment, and forecasting, making it crucial for workers to develop analytical skills and a comfort level with these technologies.

The rise of AI in the workforce also emphasizes the importance of soft skills. While technical skills are essential, the ability to collaborate, communicate effectively, and demonstrate emotional intelligence will become increasingly valuable. AI systems are not equipped to handle interpersonal dynamics or navigate complex social situations; thus, human workers will be needed to bridge the gap. Employers will likely prioritize candidates who exhibit strong soft skills alongside their technical expertise, creating a demand for a more holistic approach to workforce development.

As we embrace a future where AI plays a pivotal role in the workforce, individuals must prepare for the changes ahead. Lifelong learning will be key, as workers will need to continuously update their skills to remain relevant in an evolving job market. Additionally, fostering a mindset that embraces change and innovation will be essential. By understanding the capabilities and limitations of AI, individuals can position themselves to thrive in a world increasingly dominated by artificial intelligence, ultimately leading to a more productive and fulfilling work life.

AI and the Economy

The integration of artificial intelligence into the economy is reshaping industries and altering the landscape of work as we know it. AI technologies are enhancing productivity, streamlining operations, and driving innovation across various sectors. With capabilities such as data analysis, predictive modeling, and automation, businesses are leveraging AI to make informed decisions, optimize resource allocation, and improve customer experiences. As a result, the economic implications of AI are profound, presenting both opportunities and challenges that society must navigate.

One of the most significant impacts of AI on the economy is the transformation of the labor market. While AI can enhance efficiency and create new job opportunities in tech-driven industries, it also poses a risk of job displacement in traditional roles. As machines take over repetitive and mundane tasks, workers will need to adapt by acquiring new skills that complement AI technologies. This shift emphasizes the importance of lifelong learning and vocational training, ensuring that individuals are equipped to thrive in an AI-enhanced job market.

Small and medium-sized enterprises (SMEs) are particularly poised to benefit from AI advancements. With accessible AI tools and platforms, these businesses can harness the power of data analytics and automation without requiring significant investments. This democratization of technology enables SMEs to compete more effectively with larger corporations, fostering innovation and driving economic growth. However, it also necessitates that SMEs adopt strategic approaches to integrate AI into their operations and remain adaptable to evolving market conditions.

Investment in AI research and development is another critical aspect influencing the economy. Governments and private sectors are increasingly recognizing the potential of AI to drive economic growth, leading to substantial funding in research initiatives. This investment not only accelerates technological advancements but also encourages collaboration between academia, industry, and startups. As a result, regions that prioritize AI development may experience job creation, increased competitiveness, and overall economic resilience.

Lastly, ethical considerations surrounding AI's impact on the economy cannot be overlooked. As AI technologies become more prevalent, issues such as data privacy, algorithmic bias, and the digital divide must be addressed to ensure equitable economic outcomes. Policymakers and business leaders have a responsibility to create frameworks that promote transparency and fairness in AI deployment, fostering a sustainable economic environment. By embracing these ethical challenges, society can better prepare for an AI-driven future, ensuring that the benefits of AI are shared broadly and inclusively.

Ethical Considerations

Ethical considerations surrounding artificial intelligence are critical as society increasingly integrates AI into daily life. One of the foremost concerns is the issue of privacy. As AI systems collect vast amounts of personal data to function effectively, there is a significant risk of this information being misused or inadequately protected. Individuals may unwittingly share sensitive information, leading to potential breaches of privacy. It is essential for both developers and users of AI technologies to advocate for robust data protection measures and transparent data practices to safeguard personal information.

Another vital ethical consideration is the potential for bias in AI systems. Algorithms trained on historical data can inadvertently reflect and perpetuate existing societal biases. This can lead to unfair treatment of certain groups, particularly in areas such as hiring, law enforcement, and lending. To address this, ongoing scrutiny of AI models is necessary, alongside the implementation of diverse datasets that accurately represent the population. Inclusive practices in AI development can help mitigate bias, fostering systems that promote equality rather than reinforce discrimination.

Accountability in AI decision-making is also a pressing ethical issue. As AI systems become more autonomous, determining who is responsible for their actions becomes increasingly complex. In situations where AI performs tasks that result in harm or unintended consequences, the question of liability arises. Clear guidelines and regulatory frameworks must be established to outline accountability measures for AI developers, users, and institutions. This ensures that there are identifiable points of responsibility, which can help maintain public trust in AI technologies.

The implications of AI on employment and the workforce further complicate ethical considerations. As automation and AI technologies evolve, the potential for job displacement increases, affecting millions of workers and their families. It is crucial for stakeholders to engage in proactive discussions about workforce transition, reskilling, and the creation of new job opportunities in an AI-driven economy. By prioritizing education and training programs, society can better prepare for the changes brought about by AI, ensuring that individuals can thrive in a landscape altered by technology.

Lastly, the ethical deployment of AI technologies must consider the broader impact on society and human relationships. AI can enhance convenience and efficiency, but it can also lead to isolation and reduced human interaction. Striking a balance between leveraging AI for improvement while fostering meaningful connections among individuals is essential. Encouraging discussions around the role of AI in everyday life can help cultivate a community that values human experiences alongside technological advancements, ensuring that the integration of AI enriches rather than detracts from our social fabric.

Chapter 3: Preparing for an AI-Driven Future

Skills for the Future Workforce

As we navigate the evolving landscape shaped by artificial intelligence, it is crucial to recognize the skills that will define the future workforce. The integration of AI into various sectors necessitates a shift in the skills required for success. Many traditional roles are likely to be transformed or replaced, making adaptability a key competency. Individuals must embrace lifelong learning, staying informed about technological advancements and continuously updating their skills to remain relevant in the job market.

Technical proficiency is increasingly important in a world where AI tools are ubiquitous. Understanding how to work alongside AI systems, whether through programming, data analysis, or operating advanced software, will be critical. Workers will need to develop a foundational knowledge of AI principles, including machine learning and data processing. This technical skill set not only enhances employability but also empowers individuals to leverage AI effectively in their respective fields, whether in healthcare, finance, or creative industries.

In addition to technical skills, soft skills will play a vital role in the future workforce. Abilities such as critical thinking, creativity, and emotional intelligence will be essential as humans and machines collaborate more closely. Employers will increasingly seek individuals who can think outside the box and approach problems from innovative angles. Furthermore, emotional intelligence will aid in navigating workplace dynamics and fostering collaboration in diverse teams, ensuring that human insights complement AI capabilities.

Another important skill for the future workforce is the ability to work in interdisciplinary teams. As AI technologies permeate various sectors, professionals will need to collaborate across disciplines, combining expertise from fields such as engineering, design, and social sciences. This collaborative approach will facilitate holistic solutions to complex problems, allowing teams to harness the strengths of AI while addressing the ethical and societal implications of its deployment. An openness to diverse perspectives will be essential in creating effective strategies that consider the multifaceted nature of challenges posed by AI.

Finally, a strong ethical framework will be indispensable for individuals navigating a workforce increasingly influenced by AI. As decision-making becomes more data-driven, understanding the ethical implications of AI technologies will be paramount. Workers will need to advocate for transparency, fairness, and accountability in AI applications, ensuring that these tools are used responsibly and equitably. By cultivating a robust ethical awareness, individuals can contribute to a future workforce that not only embraces innovation but also prioritizes the well-being of society as a whole.

Lifelong Learning and Adaptability

Lifelong learning is becoming an essential paradigm in a world increasingly influenced by artificial intelligence. As AI technologies evolve, so too must our skills and knowledge. Engaging in continuous education allows individuals to stay relevant in the job market and develop the adaptability needed to navigate the complexities introduced by AI. This commitment to learning fosters resilience, enabling people to embrace change rather than resist it. By cultivating a mindset centered on lifelong learning, individuals can effectively prepare themselves for the challenges and opportunities presented by an AI-driven future.

Adaptability is closely linked to lifelong learning, as it embodies the ability to adjust to new circumstances and environments. In an era where AI systems are rapidly transforming industries, the ability to pivot and acquire new skills becomes vital. This adaptability is not merely about keeping up with technological advancements; it also involves developing critical thinking, emotional intelligence, and creativity. These human-centric skills complement AI capabilities, ensuring that individuals can work alongside machines rather than be replaced by them. By nurturing adaptability, individuals position themselves to thrive in an AI-enhanced world.

Educational institutions and organizations must also embrace lifelong learning and adaptability in their structures and curricula. Traditional educational models often focus on static knowledge acquisition, which may not suffice in a dynamic, AI-driven landscape. Instead, fostering a culture of continuous learning that encourages experimentation, collaboration, and real-world problem-solving can better equip learners for the future. This shift requires innovative teaching methods, such as project-based learning and interdisciplinary approaches, which can engage students and instill a passion for lifelong learning.

In addition to formal education, individuals can pursue learning through various informal channels, such as online courses, workshops, and community initiatives. These resources provide accessible opportunities to acquire new skills and knowledge, enabling individuals to tailor their learning experiences to their specific needs and interests. Social media and professional networks also offer platforms for sharing insights and experiences, further enhancing the learning process. By actively seeking out these opportunities, individuals can enhance their adaptability and stay informed about emerging trends and technologies.

Ultimately, embracing lifelong learning and adaptability is not just a personal endeavor; it is a collective responsibility that society must uphold. As artificial intelligence continues to reshape our lives, it is crucial to foster environments that value and promote continuous learning. This collective effort will ensure that everyone, regardless of their background or profession, can develop the skills necessary to thrive in a future where AI plays a dominant role. By prioritizing lifelong learning and adaptability, we can create a more inclusive and resilient society, capable of harnessing the full potential of artificial intelligence while mitigating its challenges.

Emotional Intelligence in an AI World

Emotional intelligence (EI) refers to the ability to recognize, understand, and manage our own emotions, as well as the emotions of others. As artificial intelligence continues to integrate into daily life, the importance of emotional intelligence becomes even more pronounced. In a world where AI can perform tasks with speed and accuracy, the human capacity for empathy, emotional awareness, and social skills sets individuals apart. This distinct advantage allows people to navigate complex interpersonal dynamics, fostering relationships that machines cannot replicate.

In an AI-driven landscape, emotional intelligence plays a vital role in human interaction, particularly in the workplace. As AI takes over routine tasks, employees will increasingly rely on their emotional intelligence to collaborate effectively, resolve conflicts, and lead teams. Organizations that prioritize EI training will cultivate a workforce capable of leveraging technology while maintaining strong interpersonal connections. This combination of technical proficiency and emotional awareness is essential for fostering innovation and creativity in a rapidly evolving environment.

Moreover, emotional intelligence aids individuals in adapting to the changes brought about by AI. As technology reshapes industries and job roles, the ability to manage stress and uncertainty becomes crucial. Those with high emotional intelligence can better cope with the emotional repercussions of job displacement or shifts in career paths, allowing them to approach transitions with resilience and openness. This adaptability is not only beneficial on a personal level but also contributes to a more stable and supportive community as people learn to navigate the challenges together.

The integration of AI into our lives also raises questions about the nature of human connection. While AI can simulate certain aspects of emotional interaction, it lacks genuine understanding and empathy. As individuals interact more with machines, it is essential to maintain a focus on developing emotional intelligence to ensure authentic relationships with one another. By prioritizing human connection and emotional awareness, society can counterbalance the potential alienation caused by increased reliance on technology, reinforcing the value of empathy in personal and professional settings.

Finally, fostering emotional intelligence in an AI world involves education and self-awareness. Schools and organizations can implement programs that emphasize emotional skills, teaching individuals how to recognize their own emotions and those of others. Mindfulness practices, communication workshops, and conflict resolution training are effective ways to enhance EI. As people become more emotionally intelligent, they not only improve their own well-being but also contribute to a compassionate society that values emotional connections in an increasingly automated world.

Chapter 4: AI in Personal Life

Smart Homes and Personal Assistants

Smart homes represent a significant evolution in how we interact with our living spaces, integrating technology to enhance comfort, security, and energy efficiency. At the heart of this transformation are personal assistants powered by artificial intelligence. These systems allow for seamless control over various household functions, from adjusting the thermostat to managing lighting and security systems. The integration of smart devices creates an ecosystem that not only simplifies daily tasks but also enables homeowners to monitor their environments in real-time, leading to more informed decisions about energy consumption and home safety.

One of the most compelling features of smart homes is their ability to learn from user behavior. Personal assistants analyze routines and preferences, adapting their responses over time to provide a more personalized experience. For instance, a smart thermostat can learn the times when occupants are typically home or away and adjust the temperature accordingly. This not only enhances comfort but can also lead to significant energy savings. As machine learning technologies continue to advance, the potential for smarter homes will expand, making them even more intuitive and responsive to individual needs.

Security is another critical aspect of smart homes, with personal assistants playing a pivotal role. These systems can monitor security cameras, detect unusual activity, and send alerts to homeowners' smartphones. Additionally, they can automate security measures, such as locking doors or turning on outdoor lights at specific times. This level of control provides peace of mind, especially for those who travel frequently or have young children at home. The integration of AI in home security systems allows for ongoing improvements in threat detection and response, making homes safer than ever.

The convenience offered by smart homes extends to everyday tasks, as personal assistants can manage shopping lists, control entertainment systems, and even schedule appointments. Voice-activated commands allow users to interact with their devices hands-free, making it easier to multitask. This capability is particularly beneficial in busy households where time is often at a premium. As these systems become more sophisticated, the range of tasks they can handle will continue to grow, further embedding them into the fabric of daily life.

While the benefits of smart homes and personal assistants are clear, there are also considerations to keep in mind. Privacy and data security are paramount, as these systems collect and process vast amounts of personal information. Users must remain vigilant about understanding how their data is used and take measures to protect their information. As we embrace the future of living with AI, it is essential to balance the convenience and efficiency of smart technology with the responsibility of safeguarding our privacy in an increasingly interconnected world.

Health and Wellness Applications

Health and wellness applications powered by artificial intelligence represent a significant advancement in personal health management. These applications range from fitness trackers to mental health support tools, offering users personalized insights and recommendations based on their unique health data. By leveraging machine learning algorithms, these apps can analyze patterns in user behavior, activity levels, and even biometric data to create tailored wellness plans that help individuals achieve their health goals more effectively.

One of the most notable benefits of AI-driven health applications is their ability to monitor and analyze health metrics in real time. For instance, apps linked to wearable devices can track heart rate, sleep quality, and physical activity. This continuous monitoring provides users with immediate feedback, enabling them to make informed decisions about their lifestyle choices. By accessing this data, users can identify trends and make adjustments to their routines that promote better overall health, thereby fostering a proactive approach to wellness.

In addition to physical health, AI applications are increasingly addressing mental health needs. Platforms that offer guided meditation, cognitive behavioral therapy exercises, and mood tracking utilize AI to adapt their content to the user's emotional state and preferences. These applications can suggest specific resources or exercises based on user interactions, making mental health support more accessible and personalized. The anonymity and convenience of these digital tools also encourage users to seek help when they might be less inclined to do so in traditional settings.

Moreover, health and wellness applications are becoming integral in managing chronic conditions. AI can assist in medication management, reminding users to take their medications on time and providing information about potential interactions. For individuals with conditions such as diabetes or hypertension, these apps can track relevant health data and alert users to concerning trends. This capability not only empowers users to take control of their health but also facilitates better communication with healthcare providers, as patients can share detailed data during consultations.

As we move forward in a world increasingly influenced by artificial intelligence, understanding how to effectively utilize these health and wellness applications will be crucial. Users must remain vigilant about data privacy and the ethical implications of sharing personal health information. By embracing these technologies while maintaining awareness of their limitations and responsibilities, individuals can enhance their health and wellness journeys, paving the way for a more informed and health-conscious society.

AI in Entertainment

AI in entertainment has transformed the way we consume media, create content, and interact with our favorite forms of artistic expression. From streaming services employing sophisticated algorithms to recommend movies and shows tailored to individual tastes, to virtual reality experiences that immerse users in interactive worlds, AI has become a vital component in shaping the entertainment landscape. This technological evolution has not only enhanced user experience but has also influenced the production processes, enabling creators to leverage data insights to craft compelling narratives that resonate with audiences.

One of the most notable applications of AI in entertainment is in the realm of content creation. Filmmakers, musicians, and writers increasingly utilize AI tools to generate ideas, draft scripts, compose music, and even edit footage. AI algorithms can analyze vast amounts of existing content to identify trends, themes, and styles that appeal to viewers or listeners. This data-driven approach allows creators to experiment with innovative concepts and push the boundaries of traditional storytelling, resulting in fresh and engaging content that captures audience attention.

Moreover, AI has revolutionized the way we experience entertainment through personalized recommendations. Streaming platforms utilize machine learning algorithms to analyze user behavior, preferences, and viewing history to suggest content that matches individual tastes. This level of personalization not only enhances user satisfaction but also increases engagement and loyalty to these platforms. Viewers can discover new shows, movies, or music that they might not have encountered otherwise, creating a more diverse and enriched entertainment experience.

In addition to content creation and personalization, AI has made significant strides in enhancing the visual and auditory aspects of entertainment. Tools powered by AI are now capable of improving video quality, generating realistic special effects, and even dubbing films in multiple languages while maintaining the actors' natural expressions and tones. This technological advancement not only streamlines production but also broadens the accessibility of entertainment by making it easier to reach global audiences. As a result, creators can share their work with diverse demographics, fostering a more inclusive entertainment culture.

As AI continues to evolve, its role in entertainment will likely expand further. Emerging technologies such as virtual reality and augmented reality are already seeing the integration of AI to create immersive experiences that blend the digital and physical worlds. This presents exciting opportunities for storytelling and audience engagement, where viewers can actively participate in narratives rather than passively observe. As we embrace this future, understanding the implications of AI in entertainment will be crucial for both creators and consumers, paving the way for a richer and more dynamic cultural landscape.

Chapter 5: Navigating Relationships with AI

AI Companionship and Social Robots

AI companionship and social robots are rapidly becoming integral parts of our daily lives, reshaping how we interact with technology and one another. These AI-driven entities are designed to provide emotional support, companionship, and social interaction, appealing to various demographics, including the elderly, children, and individuals with disabilities. The development of these technologies stems from the desire to alleviate loneliness and enhance social engagement, particularly in a world where physical interactions may be limited. As these systems become more sophisticated, they promise to redefine the boundaries of human-technology relationships.

The rise of social robots is particularly notable in the context of aging populations. Many elderly individuals experience isolation, which can lead to mental health issues. Social robots, equipped with AI, can engage in conversation, offer reminders for medication, and even encourage physical activity. These robots can serve as companions that provide not just functional support but also emotional connection, helping to bridge the gap between individuals and their loved ones. The design of these robots often incorporates elements that evoke empathy and warmth, making them more relatable and effective in their roles.

In addition to the elderly, AI companionship is gaining traction among younger generations. Children, especially those with social difficulties or developmental disorders, can benefit from interactions with social robots. These robots can provide a non-threatening environment for practicing social skills, communication, and emotional expression. They often employ gamified learning techniques, making interactions both educational and enjoyable. As children grow more accustomed to these technologies, they may develop a unique relationship with them, potentially reshaping their understanding of friendship and social dynamics.

However, the integration of AI companionship and social robots raises important ethical considerations. Questions surrounding privacy, data security, and the emotional implications of forming attachments to non-human entities must be addressed. As these technologies collect data to personalize interactions, concerns about how this information is used, stored, and protected become paramount. Additionally, there is a need for guidelines on how to foster healthy relationships between humans and robots, ensuring that these technologies enhance rather than replace human connections.

Looking toward the future, the role of AI companionship and social robots is likely to expand, driven by advancements in machine learning, natural language processing, and emotional intelligence. As society continues to embrace AI in everyday life, it will be crucial to understand the impact of these developments on human behavior and relationships. Embracing these technologies with a thoughtful approach can lead to a more connected and supportive society, where AI serves not just as a tool but as a meaningful companion in our lives.

Building Human–AI Relationships

Building human-AI relationships involves understanding the dynamics of interaction between humans and artificial intelligence systems. As AI technologies continue to evolve and integrate into various aspects of daily life, the need for healthy and constructive relationships with these systems becomes increasingly important. This relationship is not only about the functionality of AI but also encompasses emotional and social dimensions that can enhance the overall user experience.

First, it is essential to recognize the different forms of AI that people encounter. From virtual assistants like Siri and Alexa to more complex systems used in healthcare and education, AI can take many shapes. Each of these forms requires a unique approach to interaction. Users should learn how to communicate effectively with AI, understanding its capabilities and limitations. This knowledge fosters a more productive relationship, as individuals can set realistic expectations and engage with AI in a way that maximizes its potential.

Trust plays a critical role in building effective human-AI relationships. Users need to feel confident in the AI systems they interact with, particularly when it comes to sensitive areas like data privacy and security. Developers and organizations must prioritize transparency, providing clear information about how AI systems operate, the data they collect, and how that data is used. By fostering an environment of trust, users are more likely to embrace AI as a beneficial part of their lives rather than viewing it with skepticism or fear.

Another important aspect of human-AI relationships is empathy. As AI systems become more sophisticated, the ability of these systems to recognize and respond to human emotions is becoming a focus of research and development. AI that can understand and adapt to users' emotional states can create a more engaging and supportive user experience. For instance, mental health applications that utilize AI can provide personalized support, making users feel heard and understood. This emotional connection can enhance the effectiveness of AI in assisting individuals in various aspects of their lives.

Finally, fostering a collaborative mindset is crucial for building successful human-AI relationships. Rather than viewing AI as a replacement for human capabilities, it should be seen as a tool that complements and enhances human potential. Encouraging users to engage with AI in a way that emphasizes collaboration can lead to innovative solutions and improved outcomes across various fields, including business, education, and healthcare. By embracing AI as a partner, individuals can harness its strengths while leveraging their unique human abilities, ultimately leading to a more harmonious coexistence with technology.

The Role of AI in Communication

The integration of artificial intelligence into communication has transformed the way individuals and organizations interact. AI technologies, such as natural language processing and machine learning, facilitate more efficient and effective communication across various platforms. From chatbots that provide instant customer service to virtual assistants that help manage schedules and tasks, AI has made communication more accessible, timely, and personalized. These advancements not only enhance user experience but also free up human resources for more complex and creative tasks.

In personal communication, AI tools like language translation apps and speech recognition software have broken down barriers that once hindered cross-cultural interactions. With real-time translation capabilities, individuals can converse in different languages without the need for a human translator. This fosters greater understanding and collaboration among diverse groups, promoting inclusivity in both personal and professional settings. Additionally, AI-driven platforms can analyze communication patterns, offering suggestions to improve clarity and engagement, thus enhancing interpersonal relationships.

In the business realm, AI plays a crucial role in streamlining communication processes. Organizations are increasingly adopting AI-driven tools to analyze customer interactions and feedback, allowing them to tailor marketing strategies and improve customer satisfaction. AI can sift through vast amounts of data to identify trends and preferences, enabling businesses to communicate more effectively with their target audience. Furthermore, AI-powered collaboration tools facilitate remote teamwork, ensuring that employees can communicate seamlessly regardless of their physical location.

The rise of AI in communication also raises important ethical considerations. Issues such as data privacy, misinformation, and the potential for bias in AI algorithms necessitate a careful approach to how these technologies are implemented. As AI systems increasingly influence communication, it is essential for users and developers to prioritize transparency and accountability. This includes understanding how AI processes information and ensuring that the tools used are designed to promote fair and respectful communication.

As society continues to embrace AI, individuals must adapt to these changes in communication dynamics. Educating oneself about AI technologies and their implications will be crucial in navigating an AI-dominated world. By understanding the capabilities and limitations of AI in communication, individuals can leverage these tools to enhance their interactions while remaining vigilant about the ethical challenges that accompany this technological evolution. Embracing AI as a communication ally can lead to more meaningful and productive connections in both personal and professional spheres.

Chapter 6: Privacy and Security in an AI World

Data Privacy Concerns

Data privacy concerns have emerged as one of the most pressing issues in the age of artificial intelligence. As AI technologies become increasingly integrated into our daily lives, the volume of personal data collected, processed, and stored is growing exponentially. This data often includes sensitive information such as health records, financial details, and personal preferences. The more personalized our interactions with AI become, the more data we share, raising significant questions about who has access to this information and how it is being used.

One primary concern surrounding data privacy is the potential for misuse of personal information. Companies and organizations that deploy AI systems often collect data for legitimate purposes, such as improving services or enhancing user experiences. However, the risk of data breaches, hacking, and unauthorized access remains omnipresent. When sensitive data falls into the wrong hands, it can lead to identity theft, financial loss, and other significant consequences for individuals. Thus, understanding the risks associated with data sharing is crucial for anyone engaging with AI technologies.

Another aspect of data privacy concerns relates to the lack of transparency in how AI systems operate. Many AI algorithms function as "black boxes," meaning that users cannot easily discern how their data is being used or how decisions are being made. This opacity can lead to mistrust among users, who may feel that their information is being exploited without their consent. The absence of clear guidelines on data usage and retention further exacerbates this issue, creating an environment where individuals may unknowingly forfeit control over their own data.

Regulatory frameworks are beginning to emerge in response to these challenges, yet many believe that existing laws are insufficient to address the complexities of AI and data privacy. Legislation such as the General Data Protection Regulation (GDPR) in Europe has made strides in protecting consumer rights, but the rapid pace of technological advancement often outstrips the ability of lawmakers to keep up. As a result, there is a pressing need for ongoing dialogue between technologists, policymakers, and the public to develop comprehensive strategies that safeguard personal data while fostering innovation.

Ultimately, individuals must take proactive steps to protect their data in an AI-driven world. This includes being informed about privacy settings on devices and applications, understanding the implications of data sharing, and advocating for stronger privacy protections at the legislative level. By becoming more aware of data privacy concerns and taking action, individuals can help shape a future where AI serves humanity without compromising personal privacy.

Cybersecurity Challenges

The integration of artificial intelligence (AI) into everyday life has brought about significant advancements, but it has also introduced a host of cybersecurity challenges that individuals and organizations must navigate. As AI systems become more prevalent, they present new vulnerabilities that can be exploited by malicious actors. Understanding these challenges is crucial for anyone looking to live harmoniously with AI. The threat landscape is constantly evolving, and being informed is the first step in protecting oneself from potential risks.

One of the primary challenges in AI-driven environments is the sophistication of cyber attacks. Traditional methods of cybersecurity may not be sufficient against AI-powered threats that can analyze vast amounts of data and identify weaknesses in real-time. For instance, adversarial attacks involve manipulating AI algorithms to produce incorrect outputs, which can lead to severe consequences in applications such as facial recognition, autonomous vehicles, and security monitoring systems. As attackers employ more advanced techniques, it becomes essential for individuals to adopt a proactive approach to cybersecurity.

Data privacy concerns are another significant aspect of the cybersecurity challenges posed by AI. The increasing reliance on machine learning algorithms requires access to large datasets, often containing sensitive personal information. In the quest for improved AI performance, the risk of data breaches and unauthorized access to private information escalates. Individuals must be vigilant about how their data is collected, stored, and utilized, ensuring that they understand the privacy policies of the AI systems they engage with. Implementing strong data protection measures and advocating for transparent practices can help mitigate these risks.

Moreover, the potential for AI systems to be used in cyber warfare and espionage raises serious concerns about national and global security. As countries invest in AI technologies for defense and intelligence purposes, the threat of AI-driven cyber attacks becomes more pronounced. The possibility of AI being used to launch large-scale attacks on critical infrastructure, financial systems, or even democratic processes is a growing concern. This underscores the importance of international cooperation in establishing norms and regulations around the use of AI in cybersecurity, ensuring that such technologies are not weaponized against civilian populations.

Finally, the challenge of ensuring ethical AI development cannot be overlooked. The algorithms that power AI systems are inherently influenced by the data they are trained on, which can lead to biases and ethical dilemmas. Cybersecurity measures need to be designed with fairness and accountability in mind, ensuring that AI systems do not inadvertently perpetuate discrimination or harm. As AI continues to evolve, fostering a culture of ethical responsibility among developers and users alike will be crucial in addressing the cybersecurity challenges that accompany this technological shift. Engaging in open discussions about the implications of AI will empower everyone to contribute to a safer digital future.

Protecting Personal Information

In today's digital age, protecting personal information has never been more critical, particularly as artificial intelligence (AI) becomes increasingly integrated into our daily lives. With the vast amounts of data collected by AI systems, individuals must remain vigilant about safeguarding their personal details. This requires a comprehensive understanding of how personal information is gathered, processed, and used by various technologies. Knowledge of these processes empowers individuals to make informed decisions regarding their privacy and security.

One of the most significant aspects of protecting personal information involves understanding the importance of data privacy settings. Many online platforms and applications offer customizable privacy options that allow users to control what information is shared and with whom. By regularly reviewing and adjusting these settings, individuals can minimize the amount of personal data that is accessible to AI algorithms and third-party entities. This proactive approach can help reduce the risk of identity theft, data breaches, and unauthorized surveillance.

Moreover, individuals should be aware of the types of personal information that can be vulnerable to exposure. Sensitive data, such as financial information, social security numbers, and health records, should be treated with the highest level of caution. Ensuring that such information is encrypted and stored securely is essential. Additionally, understanding the implications of sharing seemingly innocuous information, like preferences or location data, can help individuals recognize the potential for misuse in conjunction with AI technologies.

Education plays a vital role in fostering a culture of data protection. Individuals must stay informed about the latest developments in AI and cybersecurity. This includes being aware of new threats, understanding the implications of emerging technologies, and recognizing the importance of digital literacy. By participating in workshops, webinars, and online courses, individuals can equip themselves with the knowledge necessary to navigate the complexities of personal information protection in an AI-driven world.

Finally, it is essential to advocate for stronger regulations and policies that protect personal information. Governments and organizations must prioritize the establishment of comprehensive frameworks that address data privacy and security concerns. By supporting initiatives aimed at enhancing data protection laws, individuals can contribute to a safer digital environment. The collaboration between citizens, technology providers, and policymakers will be crucial in ensuring that personal information remains private and secure as we embrace the future of AI.

Chapter 7: Embracing Ethical AI

Understanding AI Bias

Understanding AI bias is crucial as artificial intelligence systems increasingly influence daily life. AI bias refers to the systematic favoritism or prejudice embedded within AI algorithms, often resulting from the data upon which these systems are trained. Since AI learns from existing data, any inherent biases in that data can be perpetuated or even amplified in the outcomes generated by the AI. This can manifest in various domains, from hiring practices and loan approvals to facial recognition technologies and content recommendations.

One of the primary sources of AI bias is the data used for training the algorithms. If the data is unrepresentative of the broader population, the AI will inherently produce skewed results. For instance, if an AI model is trained predominantly on data from a specific demographic, it may make decisions that favor that group while disadvantaging others. This has significant implications, particularly in sectors such as healthcare, where biased data can lead to unequal treatment options for different demographic groups.

Moreover, bias can also creep into the design and implementation of AI systems. Developers may unintentionally introduce their own biases through the choices they make in algorithm design, feature selection, and even the interpretation of data. These biases can affect how an AI system functions and the outcomes it produces, further complicating the landscape of AI ethics and fairness. Addressing these biases requires a concerted effort from technology creators, policymakers, and society at large to ensure that AI systems are designed with inclusivity and fairness in mind.

To combat AI bias, various strategies can be employed. One effective approach is the use of diverse and representative datasets during the training phase. By ensuring that the data encompasses a wide range of perspectives and experiences, the resulting AI systems can operate more equitably. Regular audits of AI systems can also help identify and mitigate biases, allowing for continuous improvement and adaptation. Transparency in AI processes is essential, as it enables stakeholders to understand how decisions are made and to hold developers accountable for biased outcomes.

Ultimately, understanding AI bias is vital for navigating a future increasingly shaped by artificial intelligence. As individuals, we must be aware of the potential for bias in AI technologies and advocate for fairness and transparency in their development and deployment. By fostering a culture of critical engagement with AI, society can work toward harnessing the benefits of these powerful tools while minimizing the risks associated with bias, ensuring that technology serves all members of the community equitably.

Promoting Transparency and Accountability

Promoting transparency and accountability in the age of artificial intelligence is essential for fostering trust between technology providers and users. As AI systems become increasingly integrated into everyday life, the potential for misunderstanding and misuse grows. Transparency involves making the workings of AI systems clear and comprehensible to users, while accountability ensures that organizations and developers are responsible for the outcomes of their AI technologies. By advancing these principles, society can navigate the complexities of AI with greater assurance and understanding.

One key aspect of transparency is the explainability of AI algorithms. Users should be able to understand how decisions are made by AI systems, particularly in high-stakes situations such as healthcare, finance, and law enforcement. Explainable AI allows individuals to grasp the rationale behind specific outputs, which can reduce anxiety and build confidence in automated systems. Developers are increasingly called upon to create models that are not only effective but also interpretable, enabling users to engage with AI in a more informed manner.

Accountability in AI involves establishing clear guidelines and frameworks that hold developers and organizations responsible for their technology. This includes creating regulations that require companies to disclose their AI methodologies and the potential biases that may inform their algorithms. By promoting standards for ethical AI development, stakeholders can ensure that the interests of users are protected. Organizations must also implement mechanisms for redress when AI systems cause harm or produce unintended consequences, reinforcing the notion that technology should serve humanity responsibly.

The role of public awareness campaigns is vital in promoting transparency and accountability. Educating the general public about AI technologies, their benefits, and potential risks can empower individuals to make informed decisions. These initiatives can help demystify AI and encourage open discussions about ethical considerations. When users are informed, they are better equipped to question and critique the systems they interact with, leading to healthier scrutiny of AI development practices.

Finally, collaboration between various stakeholders is critical to enhancing transparency and accountability in AI. Governments, businesses, academics, and civil society must work together to establish best practices and share knowledge about ethical AI use. This collaborative approach can lead to the development of robust policies that prioritize user rights and promote ethical standards. As society embraces the integration of AI into daily life, prioritizing transparency and accountability will be fundamental to ensuring that these technologies are leveraged for the greater good, paving the way for a more equitable and informed future.

The Role of Policy and Regulation

The integration of artificial intelligence into everyday life has necessitated a comprehensive approach to policy and regulation. As AI technologies advance, they present both opportunities and challenges that require careful consideration from lawmakers and regulatory bodies. The role of policy and regulation is crucial in ensuring that AI is developed and deployed in ways that are ethical, safe, and beneficial for society. Policymakers must navigate the complexities of a rapidly evolving technological landscape while addressing concerns related to privacy, security, and equity.

One of the primary responsibilities of policy and regulation is to establish frameworks that guide the ethical use of AI. This involves setting standards for transparency, accountability, and fairness in AI systems. Regulations can help mitigate biases that may be inherent in algorithms, ensuring that AI applications do not perpetuate discrimination or inequality. By fostering an environment of trust, well-crafted policies can encourage public acceptance of AI technologies and their integration into various aspects of life, from healthcare to education and beyond.

Furthermore, regulations play a significant role in safeguarding individual privacy. With AI systems often relying on vast amounts of personal data, the potential for misuse or unauthorized access to this information is a critical concern. Policies that prioritize data protection are essential in empowering individuals to maintain control over their personal information. Regulations, such as data minimization and user consent requirements, can help create a balance between innovation and privacy, allowing for the responsible advancement of AI technologies.

In addition to ethical considerations, there is a growing need for regulations that address the economic implications of AI. As automation and AI-driven innovations reshape industries, there are concerns about job displacement and the future of work. Policymakers must consider strategies to support workforce transition, such as reskilling programs and social safety nets. By proactively addressing these economic challenges through targeted regulations, societies can better prepare for a future where AI plays an integral role in various sectors.

Ultimately, the role of policy and regulation in the age of AI extends beyond immediate concerns. It sets the groundwork for a sustainable and equitable relationship between humanity and technology. Effective policies can guide research and development in AI, ensuring that advancements align with societal values and priorities. As we embrace tomorrow and adapt to a world influenced by artificial intelligence, the collaborative efforts of governments, industry leaders, and the public will be essential in shaping a future that leverages AI for the common good.

Chapter 8: The Future of AI

Emerging Technologies

Emerging technologies are reshaping the landscape of our daily lives, particularly through the integration of artificial intelligence. As AI becomes more prevalent, it is essential to understand the innovations driving this transformation. From machine learning algorithms that improve decision-making to natural language processing tools that facilitate human-computer interaction, these advancements are not only enhancing efficiency but also creating new possibilities for how we live, work, and communicate. By recognizing these technologies, individuals can better prepare for a future where AI plays a central role.

One of the most significant emerging technologies is the Internet of Things (IoT), which connects everyday devices to the internet, allowing them to collect and share data. This connectivity enables smarter homes, where appliances can communicate with each other and with users, optimizing energy consumption and improving convenience. For instance, smart thermostats learn user preferences and adjust settings automatically, providing comfort while reducing energy costs. As IoT continues to evolve, individuals can expect an increasingly interconnected environment that enhances their quality of life and productivity.

Another crucial development is the advancement of robotics, which is becoming more sophisticated and versatile. Robots are not only used in industrial settings for manufacturing but are also making their way into homes and healthcare. Personal assistant robots can help with household chores, while robotic systems in hospitals can assist with surgeries or patient care. This shift towards automation is not just about replacing human labor; it is also about augmenting human capabilities, allowing people to focus on more complex tasks while robots handle repetitive or dangerous work. Understanding the role of robotics will be vital for individuals as they navigate a future with these intelligent machines.

Artificial intelligence is also driving innovations in data analysis and decision-making processes across various sectors. Big data analytics enables organizations to sift through vast amounts of information, identifying trends and insights that can inform strategies and improve outcomes. For individuals, this means more personalized services, whether in healthcare, finance, or entertainment. AI-driven recommendations can provide tailored experiences, enhancing user satisfaction and engagement. As this technology advances, consumers will need to become more adept at interpreting the implications of data-driven solutions in their lives.

Lastly, ethical considerations surrounding emerging technologies must be addressed as society embraces AI. Issues such as data privacy, security, and algorithmic bias are critical as AI systems become more integrated into daily life. Awareness of these challenges is essential for individuals to advocate for responsible AI use and to make informed choices about the technologies they adopt. By fostering a dialogue about ethics in technology, we can encourage the development of systems that prioritize human values and contribute positively to society, ensuring that the benefits of AI are realized equitably and sustainably.

Predictions for AI Development

The future of artificial intelligence (AI) development is poised to reshape numerous aspects of daily life, influencing everything from the way we work to how we interact with each other. Predictions suggest that AI will become increasingly integrated into everyday tasks, automating routine processes and enhancing productivity. This integration is likely to lead to a significant transformation in various industries, including healthcare, finance, and education, where AI can streamline operations, improve decision-making, and provide personalized experiences for users.

One of the most notable predictions for AI development is the advancement of natural language processing (NLP) technologies. As these technologies evolve, they will enable more sophisticated interactions between humans and machines. This could manifest in improved virtual assistants that understand context and nuance, allowing for more meaningful conversations. Additionally, advancements in NLP may empower individuals to access information and services more efficiently, breaking down language barriers and democratizing knowledge across different demographics.

Another critical area of development is the ethical and regulatory landscape surrounding AI. As AI systems become more prevalent, there will be an increasing demand for frameworks that ensure responsible use and accountability. Predictions indicate that governments and organizations will prioritize establishing guidelines that address privacy, bias, and security concerns. This regulatory environment will be essential for fostering public trust in AI technologies, enabling users to embrace these innovations without fearing potential negative consequences.

The role of AI in education is also expected to undergo significant changes. Predictive analytics and personalized learning platforms will likely become commonplace, catering to individual learning styles and paces. This shift could lead to improved educational outcomes and greater accessibility for students worldwide. Educators will need to adapt their teaching methods and curricula to incorporate AI tools effectively, ensuring that they enhance rather than replace traditional learning experiences.

Lastly, the job market will experience notable shifts as AI technologies advance. While some jobs may become obsolete due to automation, new roles focused on AI oversight, development, and maintenance will emerge. It is predicted that the workforce will need to adapt by acquiring new skills to thrive in this evolving landscape. Lifelong learning will become essential, as individuals seek to stay relevant and competitive in an AI-driven economy. By preparing for these changes, everyone can position themselves to not only coexist with AI but also to harness its potential for personal and societal growth.

Preparing for Change

As artificial intelligence continues to evolve and integrate into various aspects of daily life, it is essential for individuals and communities to prepare for the changes that this technology brings. Understanding how AI will influence jobs, education, and personal interactions is critical for adapting to a future where AI plays a significant role. By acknowledging these changes early on, we can develop strategies that allow us to leverage AI's benefits while minimizing potential challenges.

One of the primary areas where AI will have a profound impact is in the workforce. Many industries are experiencing automation, which can lead to job displacement but also creates opportunities for new roles that require human oversight and creativity. Preparing for this shift involves upskilling and reskilling, focusing on acquiring competencies that complement AI technologies. Educational programs and vocational training should emphasize critical thinking, emotional intelligence, and problem-solving skills, which are less likely to be automated and more valuable in an AI-driven economy.

In addition to workforce changes, AI's influence on education cannot be overstated. Personalized learning experiences powered by AI can help students learn at their own pace and cater to their unique strengths and weaknesses. However, educators and parents must be proactive in understanding the tools available and integrating them into curricula effectively. This preparation includes advocating for digital literacy and ensuring that students are equipped to navigate a world where AI is prevalent, fostering a generation that is not only consumers of technology but also critical thinkers and innovators.

Social interactions will also transform as AI systems become more integrated into everyday life. From virtual assistants to social robots, the way we connect with technology will shape our relationships and communication styles. It is crucial to establish a balance between embracing these advancements and maintaining genuine human interactions. Preparing for this change requires fostering awareness of how AI affects our social dynamics and encouraging open discussions about the ethical implications of relying on AI in personal and professional relationships.

Finally, as we prepare for a future dominated by AI, it is vital to cultivate a mindset of adaptability and resilience. Embracing change means being open to continuous learning and developing a proactive approach toward technology. Engaging in community discussions, participating in workshops, and staying informed about advancements in AI will empower individuals to navigate the complexities of this new landscape effectively. By preparing ourselves and our communities for the inevitable changes brought by AI, we can ensure a future that not only embraces innovation but also prioritizes human values and connections.

Chapter 9: Living Harmoniously with AI

Finding Balance in Technology Use

Finding balance in technology use is essential as we navigate a world increasingly influenced by artificial intelligence. The rapid integration of AI into daily life offers numerous conveniences, but it can also lead to challenges related to over-dependence and the erosion of personal interactions. Striking a balance means recognizing the role of technology in enhancing our lives while remaining mindful of its potential drawbacks. This balance allows individuals to harness the benefits of AI without compromising their well-being or relationships.

One of the first steps toward achieving balance is setting clear boundaries around technology usage. Establishing specific times for engaging with devices can help create a healthier relationship with technology. For instance, designating tech-free zones or times during meals, family gatherings, or before bedtime encourages face-to-face interactions and fosters deeper connections. These boundaries are crucial in preventing the encroachment of technology into all aspects of life, allowing individuals to enjoy the advantages AI offers without becoming overwhelmed.

Another important aspect of finding balance involves critical engagement with technology. This means being mindful of how and why we use AI tools. Instead of passively consuming information or allowing algorithms to dictate our choices, individuals should strive to actively engage with technology. This could involve questioning the sources of information, understanding the algorithms that shape our online experiences, and making informed decisions about which AI applications to incorporate into our daily routines. By cultivating this critical mindset, users can better navigate the digital landscape and make choices that align with their values and needs.

Moreover, fostering a culture of digital literacy within communities can enhance collective understanding of technology's role in our lives. Educational initiatives that promote skills in evaluating digital content, understanding data privacy, and using AI responsibly can empower individuals to engage thoughtfully with technology. This shared knowledge creates an environment where people can support one another in finding balance, discussing challenges, and sharing strategies for responsible technology use. Such community-driven efforts can mitigate feelings of isolation that often accompany excessive technology use.

In conclusion, finding balance in technology use is not merely a personal endeavor but a societal necessity as we embrace a future shaped by AI. By setting boundaries, engaging critically with technology, and fostering digital literacy in our communities, we can create a healthier relationship with the tools that increasingly define our lives. Embracing tomorrow means not only leveraging the advantages of AI but also ensuring that technology serves to enhance our human experience rather than diminish it. Through conscious effort and collaboration, we can navigate the complexities of technology use and cultivate a balanced, fulfilling life in an AI-driven world.

Cultivating a Positive Mindset

Cultivating a positive mindset is essential in navigating a world increasingly influenced by artificial intelligence. As AI technologies continue to evolve and integrate into daily life, individuals must adapt to these changes with an optimistic outlook. This entails recognizing the opportunities presented by AI rather than focusing solely on perceived threats. By fostering a positive mindset, individuals can engage with AI developments constructively, enhancing personal growth and well-being.

One of the first steps in cultivating a positive mindset is to embrace change as a constant in life. AI is reshaping various aspects of society, from how we work to how we communicate.

Acknowledging that change can lead to growth allows individuals to approach AI advancements with curiosity rather than fear. Embracing this perspective encourages a proactive attitude, prompting individuals to seek out learning opportunities related to AI and technology, thus empowering them to adapt more effectively.

Another important aspect is focusing on solutions instead of problems. When faced with challenges brought about by AI, such as job displacement or privacy concerns, it is crucial to shift the focus toward developing strategies that can address these issues. This solution-oriented mindset fosters resilience and creativity, enabling individuals to think critically about how to leverage AI for their benefit. By viewing challenges as opportunities for innovation, people can actively contribute to shaping a future where AI serves as a tool for enhancement rather than a source of anxiety.

Building a supportive community plays a significant role in maintaining a positive mindset in the context of AI. Engaging with others who share a similar outlook can provide encouragement and inspiration. This community can be a source of shared knowledge, where individuals exchange ideas about how to thrive in an AI-driven world. By collaborating and discussing experiences, individuals can cultivate a collective sense of optimism, reinforcing the belief that they can navigate the changes together.

Finally, practicing gratitude and mindfulness can significantly enhance one's mindset. Regularly reflecting on the positive aspects of life, including the benefits brought by AI, can shift attention away from negativity. Mindfulness practices, such as meditation or journaling, can help individuals stay grounded and present, allowing them to appreciate the advancements in technology that improve quality of life. By cultivating these habits, individuals can develop a resilient, positive mindset that not only helps them cope with the challenges of AI but also empowers them to embrace the future with enthusiasm.

Community Engagement and Collaboration

Community engagement and collaboration play a vital role in shaping the future of AI integration in our daily lives. As artificial intelligence technologies become increasingly prevalent, it is essential for individuals and communities to actively participate in discussions about their implementation and impact. Engaging with local organizations, tech developers, and educators fosters a collaborative environment where diverse perspectives can be shared. This engagement not only enhances public understanding of AI but also empowers communities to have a say in how these technologies are utilized in their environments.

One effective way to promote community engagement is through workshops and public forums that focus on AI literacy. These events can provide participants with foundational knowledge about AI, its capabilities, and its limitations. By creating a space for open dialogue, individuals can express their concerns, ask questions, and explore the ethical implications of AI technologies. Such interactions enable people to better understand how AI affects various aspects of society, including employment, privacy, and accessibility, fostering a more informed citizenry that can advocate for responsible AI use.

Collaboration between communities and technology developers is crucial for creating AI solutions that are relevant and beneficial to local needs. When developers actively seek input from community members, they can design AI systems that address specific challenges faced by those communities. This approach not only enhances the effectiveness of the technology but also builds trust between developers and users. By prioritizing local insights, AI can be tailored to support education, healthcare, and other vital services, ensuring that its impact is both positive and inclusive.

Moreover, partnerships between educational institutions and local organizations can enhance AI literacy and skills development. Schools and universities can collaborate with community groups to offer training programs that equip individuals with the skills needed to navigate an AI-driven world. By fostering a culture of lifelong learning, communities can prepare their members to adapt to technological changes and seize opportunities that AI presents.

These initiatives can help bridge the digital divide, ensuring that all individuals have access to the resources necessary to thrive in an increasingly automated society.

Finally, fostering a sense of community around AI can help mitigate fears and apprehensions associated with its rise. By creating spaces where individuals can share experiences and concerns, communities can collectively work towards solutions that prioritize human values and ethical considerations. Encouraging transparency and accountability from AI developers and policymakers is essential in this endeavor. Ultimately, through active community engagement and collaboration, society can embrace the potential of AI while ensuring that its development aligns with the collective interests and well-being of all individuals.

Chapter 10: Action Steps for Today

Setting Personal Goals

Setting personal goals in a world increasingly influenced by artificial intelligence is essential for navigating the complexities of modern life. As AI continues to reshape various aspects of daily routines, understanding how to define and pursue personal objectives becomes crucial. Goals provide direction and motivation, allowing individuals to harness the advantages of AI while minimizing potential challenges. By setting clear, achievable goals, individuals can ensure that they remain proactive in their personal and professional lives amid rapid technological changes.

To begin setting personal goals, individuals should start with self-reflection. Understanding one's values, interests, and strengths is fundamental to establishing meaningful objectives. In a world where AI can handle repetitive tasks and provide data-driven insights, individuals must identify areas where they want to grow or improve. This process may involve assessing personal aspirations, such as advancing in a career, pursuing new skills, or fostering relationships. Recognizing what truly matters enables individuals to align their goals with their authentic selves, leading to greater satisfaction and fulfillment.

Once individuals have identified their core values and interests, they can employ the SMART criteria to articulate their goals. SMART stands for Specific, Measurable, Achievable, Relevant, and Time-bound. By applying this framework, individuals can create goals that are clear and structured. For example, rather than setting a vague goal of "getting better at technology," one might set a specific goal of "completing an online course in data analytics within three months." This clarity not only enhances motivation but also allows for tracking progress, making adjustments as needed, and celebrating milestones along the way.

Incorporating AI tools into the goal-setting process can further enhance the effectiveness of personal objectives. Various applications and platforms can aid individuals in monitoring their progress, providing reminders, and facilitating accountability. AI can also offer personalized recommendations based on an individual's goals, helping to identify potential resources or strategies that align with their aspirations. By leveraging these technological advancements, individuals can streamline their efforts and stay organized, ultimately increasing their chances of success.

Finally, it is important to remain adaptable in the face of evolving circumstances. The rapid pace of change in technology and society means that personal goals may need to be adjusted over time. Regularly revisiting and reassessing goals ensures they remain relevant and aligned with current desires and opportunities. By embracing flexibility, individuals can navigate the complexities of living with AI, allowing for growth and adaptation in a world where change is the only constant. Setting personal goals, therefore, becomes not just a framework for achievement but a vital strategy for thriving in an AI-driven future.

Building a Support Network

Building a support network is essential for navigating the complexities of a world increasingly influenced by artificial intelligence. As AI technologies evolve, they can significantly alter how we work, learn, and interact. Establishing a robust support network helps individuals adapt to these changes, share experiences, and access valuable resources. It fosters a sense of community and provides a platform for collaboration and knowledge sharing, which are crucial in an era where AI can disrupt traditional roles and industries.

One effective way to build a support network is through local community groups and organizations focused on technology and AI. These groups often host workshops, discussions, and seminars that not only educate members about emerging technologies but also create opportunities for networking. Participating in these events allows individuals to meet like-minded people, exchange ideas, and form connections that can lead to collaborations or mentorships. Engaging with local initiatives can also help individuals feel more grounded and informed about the changes happening in their environments.

Online platforms play a pivotal role in creating support networks, particularly for those who may have limited access to local resources. Social media, forums, and professional networking sites can connect individuals across the globe who are navigating similar challenges related to AI. By joining relevant groups or communities, individuals can share their experiences, seek advice, and stay updated on the latest trends and tools. These digital spaces often provide a wealth of information and support, making it easier to adapt to the ongoing technological shifts.

In addition to community and online resources, educational institutions and corporate training programs can be vital in building a support network. Many universities and organizations offer courses and workshops on AI literacy, which not only enhance individual skills but also create opportunities for networking. Engaging with peers and instructors in these settings can lead to lasting professional relationships and friendships. Moreover, these environments often encourage collaborative projects, allowing participants to work together and learn from one another, further strengthening their support networks.

Lastly, fostering a culture of open communication within personal and professional circles is crucial. Encouraging discussions about the implications of AI, sharing concerns and successes, and being open to feedback can enhance relationships and build trust. This openness will allow individuals to navigate the complexities of AI together, offering support and guidance as needed. Establishing a support network rooted in collaboration and communication enables everyone to embrace the future with confidence, ensuring they are equipped to handle the challenges and opportunities that AI presents.

Staying Informed and Engaged

Staying informed and engaged in a world increasingly influenced by artificial intelligence is essential for everyone. As AI continues to evolve, its applications permeate various aspects of daily life, from personal assistants that simplify tasks to algorithms that shape our online experiences. Understanding the tools and technologies that drive these changes allows individuals to navigate this AI-driven landscape with confidence and awareness. By actively seeking knowledge about AI and its implications, people can better prepare for the future and leverage these advancements to enhance their lives.

One effective way to stay informed is to actively follow reputable sources of information on AI technology and its advancements. This includes subscribing to newsletters, reading articles from trusted publications, and following thought leaders in the AI field on social media. Engaging with a diverse array of perspectives helps individuals develop a well-rounded understanding of AI's potential benefits and challenges. Additionally, participating in online forums or local meetups can provide opportunities to discuss AI-related topics with others, fostering a community of learners who can share resources and insights.

Educational institutions and organizations are increasingly offering courses and workshops focused on AI and its applications. Taking advantage of these opportunities can deepen understanding and equip individuals with the skills needed to thrive in an AI-integrated world. Online platforms provide access to a wealth of resources, including tutorials, webinars, and interactive courses. Engaging with these materials not only enhances knowledge but also builds practical skills that can be applied in various professional and personal contexts, making individuals more competitive in the job market.

Moreover, staying engaged with AI extends beyond mere knowledge acquisition; it involves active participation in discussions about ethical considerations and societal impacts. As AI systems become more prevalent, questions surrounding privacy, security, and bias become increasingly important. Engaging in conversations about these issues is crucial for ensuring that AI development aligns with societal values and benefits all individuals. By voicing concerns and advocating for responsible AI practices, individuals can influence how AI technologies are designed and implemented, contributing to a more equitable future.

Lastly, cultivating a mindset of adaptability is vital in an era where technological advancements are rapid and often unpredictable. Being open to learning new skills and adapting to changing circumstances will enable individuals to thrive in a landscape shaped by AI. Embracing change, rather than resisting it, allows for personal and professional growth. By remaining informed and engaged, individuals can not only navigate the challenges posed by AI but also harness its potential to improve their lives, ultimately embracing a future filled with possibilities.